18.95

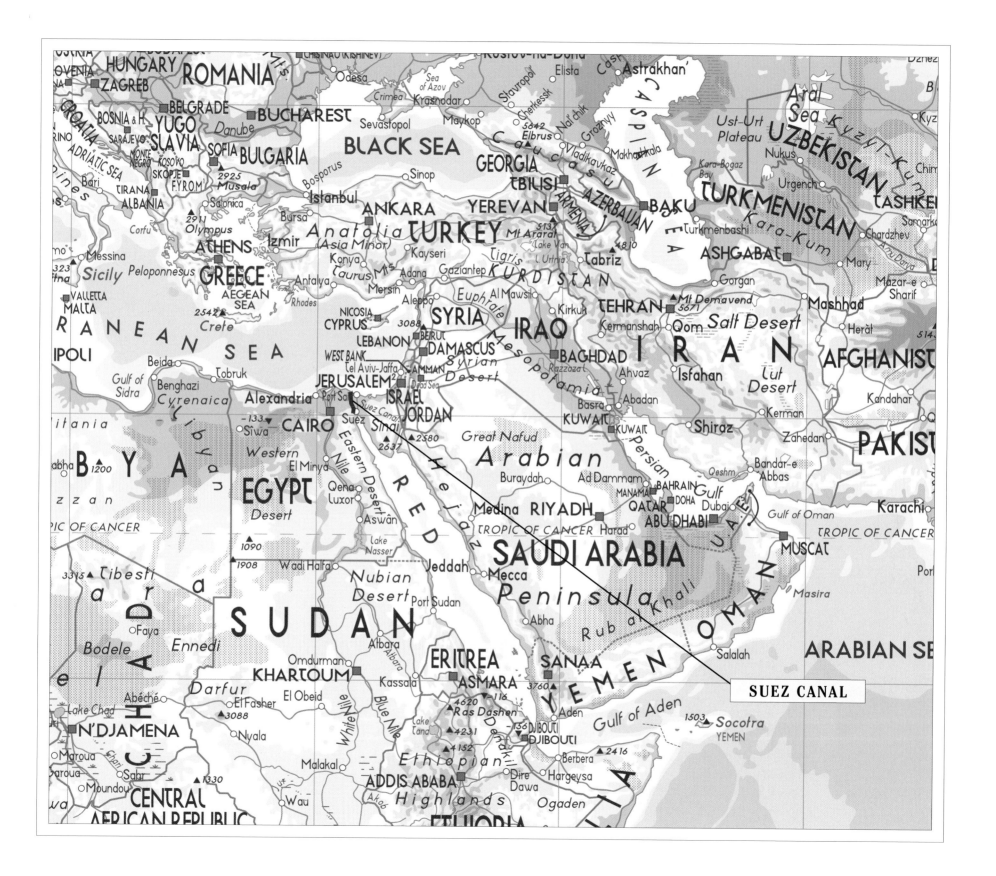

SUEZ CANAL

Published by Creative Education
123 South Broad Street, Mankato, Minnesota 56001
Creative Education is an imprint of The Creative Company.

Designed by Stephanie Blumenthal
Production design by Melinda Belter
Art direction by Rita Marshall

Photographs by Alamy (AA World Travel Library, Joe Baraban, Rob Bartee, BennettPhoto, G P Bowater,
Ian M Butterfield, bygonetimes, Christine Osborne Pictures, Reinhard Dirscherl, Kenneth Dyer, Vick Fisher,
foodfolio, Holt Studios International Ltd, ImageState, James Davis Photography, J Marshall – Tribaleye Images,
Mary Evans Picture Library, Network Photographers, North Wind Picture Archives, Lauri Nykopp, Papilio, PCL,
Nicholas Pitt, POPPERFOTO, Profimedia.CZ s.r.o., Robert Harding Picture Library Ltd, Jeff Rotman, SCPhotos,
STOCKFOLIO, B. Mete Uz, V&A Images, Colin Walton, Worldwide Picture Library), Art Resource, NY (Erich
Lessing, Réunion des Musées Nationaux), Design Maps, Inc., Getty Images (Scott Nelson, Upperhall Ltd)

Printed in the United States of America

Library of Congress Cataloging-in-Publication Data
Bodden, Valerie.
Suez Canal / by Valerie Bodden.
p. cm. — (Modern wonders of the world)
Includes index.
ISBN-13: 978-1-58341-441-5
1. Suez Canal (Egypt)—Juvenile literature. 2. Canals—Egypt—Juvenile literature. I. Title. II. Series.

HE543.B63 2006   386'.43'09—dc22   2005050670

First edition

2 4 6 8 9 7 5 3 1

SUEZ CANAL

AUTHOR
Valerie Bodden

MODERN WONDERS
— OF THE WORLD —

CREATIVE ☾ EDUCATION

Although man-made, the Suez Canal evokes a sense of natural beauty as it flows through once-barren lands. Since its opening, the great waterway has drawn ships—and people—to the desert.

Where **East** meets **West**, a strange scene rises from the shimmering heat of the desert. Huge oceanliners parade through the golden sand, one after another. There is no water in sight. And yet the ships move forward, slowly, gracefully, leaving in their wake only more sand. Seeming at first glance to be a mirage, the Suez Canal cuts through more than 100 miles (160 km) of Egyptian desert, its blue waters hidden behind hills of sand. Up and down its western shore, trees, flowers, and even towns flourish where once there had been nothing. And along its length, two worlds have been connected for more than a century.

At the time the Suez Canal was built, in the mid-19th century, there was a great fascination with engineering and technological achievements, such as bridges, railroads, and canals. As a result, construction of the Suez Canal received worldwide press coverage, with people carefully following newspaper reports of its progress.

CROSSROADS OF THE WORLD

During the more than six centuries of the Roman occupation, trade flourished in Egypt, with merchants from East and West traveling through the country—both overland and along the ancient canal—on a daily basis. Many of the merchants carried Roman coins to facilitate transactions.

Situated between Europe and Asia, Egypt has long been a natural crossroads for world trade. The first attempts at a canal, or man-made waterway, to improve travel through the hot desert sands of this country were made more than 4,000 years ago by the **pharaohs**. The canal of the pharaohs led from the Red Sea north and west to an ancient, now-dry branch of the Nile River, which flowed into the Mediterranean Sea. It was well-traveled by Egyptian traders for more than 1,000 years, but eventually strong desert winds piled sand in the canal, and it fell into disuse. In the seventh century B.C., the pharaoh Necho

II tried to rebuild the canal, but his efforts were unsuccessful.

As Egypt was conquered over the following centuries by the **Persians**, Romans, and **Muslims**, various rulers reopened the canal. During the Roman occupation of Egypt—from about 30 B.C. to A.D. 639—especially, the canal was a success. Exotic animals such as tigers and leopards, luxurious textiles such as wool and silk, and foreign spices such as cloves and ginger made their way from the Orient to Europe in exchange for gold. Soon, however, the canal was again abandoned. As trade began to move overland in camel caravans

As the Romans grew wealthier, their demand for goods such as cloves (top left) from Indonesia, ginger (bottom left) from India, rugs (top right) from Persia, and silk (bottom right) from China increased. Many of these items were transported along the ancient Egyptian canal on their way to Rome.

In 1857, Indian troops revolted against British forces occupying their country, and British reinforcements had to be "rushed" around the Cape of Good Hope, a journey that took four months. Eventually, Britain begged for permission to send troops overland through Egypt.

Both overland trade routes and sea routes around the Cape of Good Hope (opposite) proved to be dangerous and slow.

and, later, by ship around the Cape of Good Hope at the southern tip of Africa, the canal was buried by sand and remained forgotten for more than 1,000 years.

In 1832, Ferdinand de Lesseps, a French **diplomat** and engineer in the Egyptian capital of Cairo, read about the discovery of traces of the ancient canal. It sparked in him the desire to create a modern canal that would provide a direct connection between East and West, cutting 5,800 miles (9,300 km) off of the then-current shipping route from Europe to India via the Cape of Good Hope. It was a desire

that would stay with de Lesseps over the next 20 years as he was sent to different posts around the world.

Finally, in 1854, the time was right for de Lesseps to act on his idea. Mohammed Said, whom de Lesseps knew well, had recently become Egyptian **viceroy**, and de Lesseps believed that Said might approve the construction of a canal through his country. Events in the outside world were also in de Lesseps's favor. The **Industrial Revolution** had recently swept through Europe, creating the need for more raw materials from the East to supply

In the mid-19th century, the French had a passion for all things Egyptian—from **Bedouins** to pyramids. This helped Ferdinand de Lesseps sell half of the shares in the Suez Canal Company to the French public. Most of the remaining shares were sold to Egypt.

Ferdinand de Lesseps (right) knew that a canal through Egypt would bring modern importance to a country known for its ancient artifacts.

new factories. In addition, new ships were being built of iron, rather than wood, and powered by steam, rather than sail, making possible the transport of heavier goods such as iron from the East. A canal through Egypt would allow for faster and easier transport of such goods.

In November 1854, de Lesseps presented his plan for the canal to Said, who approved it immediately. Construction couldn't begin right away, however. Since Egypt was part of the **Ottoman Empire**, permission for the canal also needed to be obtained from the sultan, or ruler, of Turkey, who was heavily influenced by the British.

The British opposed the idea of a canal because they controlled the sea lanes between Europe and India. They feared that a canal would give other nations an opportunity to take the lead in Eastern trade.

Besides dealing with the sultan, de Lesseps had to find a way to finance the canal. Always inventive, he decided to sell **shares** in the new Suez Canal Company, which was created to construct and operate the waterway. In April 1859, after having raised only half of the estimated $40 million he needed, and without permission from the Ottoman Empire, de Lesseps began construction on his dream.

JOINING EAST AND WEST

The **Isthmus** of Suez, a narrow strip of land that separates the Mediterranean Sea in the north from the Red Sea in the south, is situated near the eastern border of Egypt. The populous Nile delta—the fertile area in northern Egypt where the Nile River empties into the Mediterranean Sea—lies to its west. To its east is the rugged wilderness of the Sinai Peninsula, a small desert linking Asia and Africa.

Unlike previous canals, today's Suez Canal does not flow west to link up with the Nile, but rather travels completely down the 100-mile-long (160 km) isthmus. Rather than one long, continuous waterway, the canal is actually a series of channels connecting five desert lakes. By using these lakes—four of which were dry at the time of construction—the canal's engineers ensured that less than half of the waterway's distance would have to be dug from the sand. Even with the inclusion of the lakes, however, hundreds of millions of tons of sand still had to be excavated before ships could sail through the desert.

The daunting task of removing so much sand was begun in the spring of 1859 with little more than the bare hands of 150 Egyptian laborers. Using shovels and baskets, they dug a narrow canal,

While farms dot the countryside of the Nile delta (top) to the west of the Isthmus of Suez, only a few Bedouins populate the Sinai Peninsula (bottom) to its east. South of the isthmus, the Red Sea is filled with marine life, as well as numerous shipwrecks (opposite) both ancient and modern.

While most of the Suez Canal was dug by hand or with machinery, the Shallufa Ridge, a 5-mile-long (8 km), 30-foot-high (10 m) rock outcropping, was dynamited. Two other ridges were cut through with picks, shovels, and machinery.

Sun-baked mud formed solid surfaces that early workers on the Suez Canal used as supply roads. Today, dredgers (opposite, at right) move along the waterway to areas that need to be deepened.

beginning at Lake Manzala near the Mediterranean. This shallow, marshy lake was the only one of the five desert lakes that wasn't dry. In order to create a navigable waterway through it, workers scooped mud from the lake bottom, hugged it against their chests to wring out the water, then piled it on either side of the channel they were forming. As the mud dried in the sun, it became rock-hard, forming strong embankments that could be used as roads to carry supplies. The narrow waterway that was created between the embankments was used to float heavier supplies southward.

As work progressed south of Lake Manzala, laborers continued to hand-excavate the desert. By 1862, they had made impressive progress, but at the rate they were able to dig by hand, it would have taken 15 to 20 years to complete the canal. Finally, in 1864, de Lesseps had enough money to bring in large machinery. A huge fleet of dredgers (boats and barges equipped to dig underwater) and excavators (machines used to dig from land) was built to complete the project. De Lesseps also sent large crews with machinery to the southern end of the canal to begin digging northward from the Red Sea.

In the early stages of construction, Egyptian peasants—including young children—were forced to work on the Suez Canal as a form of tax. It is estimated that thousands died, victims of heat, overwork, and **cholera**. By 1864, public outcry had brought an end to the practice of forced labor.

While the canal was being dug, new towns and harbors were being built up and down its western shore, bringing life to the barren desert. An artificial harbor was created at Port Said in the north, while the elegant town of Ismailia was built on Lake Timsah at the canal's halfway point. Where once there had been only sand, acacia and orange trees were introduced, gardens of exotic flowers were planted, and pelicans and flamingoes made their homes. A small waterway called the Sweet Water Canal was dug from the Nile River to the western shore of the Suez Canal to supply the area with fresh water.

Finally, after 10 years of construction, the Suez Canal opened to the world in November 1869. On its opening day, the canal was 100 miles (160 km) long, 26 feet (8 m) deep, and 175 feet (53 m) wide at the surface. The entire project had cost almost $100 million—more than twice the original estimate—and around 2.4 million Egyptians had worked on it, as many as 35,000 toiling under the desert sun at a time.

Before the Sweet Water Canal (bottom) was dug, camels carried fresh water to stations along the Suez Canal (top). Today, the land around the Sweet Water Canal is some of the most fertile in the world and supports fruits such as oranges (opposite center), while the water-ways support such wildlife as flamingoes (opposite far left).

TRADE AND TROUBLES

By helping to finance the Suez Canal, Egyptian rulers Mohammed Said and Ismail Pasha brought financial ruin to their country. When construction on the canal began, Egypt was debt-free. By 1875, the country owed more than $300 million to European bankers, much of it for the purchase of shares in the canal.

The Suez Canal's opening ceremony on November 17, 1869, was an elaborate affair at which ships from almost every seafaring nation in the world were present. As cannons blasted, bands played, and crowds cheered, dignitaries from around the world set sail down the new waterway from Port Said. When they reached the city of Suez at the canal's southern end, the ships were greeted by crowds celebrating their successful journey.

With the grand opening of the canal, an ancient trade route between East and West was reestablished. In increasing quantities, raw materials from the Orient made their way to Europe. No longer did goods shipped from the East include only luxury items such as silk; now, important materials such as iron ore, **copra**, and cotton were transferred to Europe via the Suez Canal. Finished products such as clothing and railroad tracks traveled from European factories back to the East.

Despite its success in reviving East-West commerce, the Suez Canal was soon the site of conflict. Almost immediately after its completion, the canal was taken out of Egyptian hands when the country's shares in the Suez Canal Company were bought by Britain. Then, in 1882, Egyptian army offi-

Since the opening of the Suez Canal, Port Said— named after viceroy Mohammed Said—has become a busy center of trade, with local vendors (opposite) offering all kinds of useful wares. The city also boasts beautiful buildings such as the Suez Canal House (top) and the Port Said lighthouse (bottom).

Even while the Suez Canal was closed from 1967 to 1975, it continued to influence worldwide shipping. Because the canal was unavailable, new, huge oil tankers were designed to make the journey around the Cape of Good Hope.

Although the Suez Canal can today hold large ships, it cannot yet accommodate the world's biggest oil tankers, designed when the canal was closed and the region heavily guarded (right).

cers led a revolt to overthrow the country's new ruler, Tawfiq Pasha. Claiming to want to protect the Egyptian government, Britain invaded Egypt and put down the rebellion. For almost 75 years, British troops remained in Egypt, securing the canal for their country. The British military finally left the country in 1956, and the Egyptian government then used its own soldiers to assume control of the Suez Canal Company and the canal itself.

Over the years, the Suez Canal has been closed several times due to armed conflicts in the area. During World Wars I and II, the canal was closed for brief periods of time. It was closed again for several months follow-ing the 1956 Suez Crisis in which Egypt fought against Israel, Britain, and France. The canal closed for eight years following the 1967 Six-Day War, a conflict between Israel and the allied countries of Egypt, Jordan, and Syria. Since 1975, the canal has remained open.

Since its opening, the Suez Canal has continuously been enlarged to accommo-date bigger and bigger ships. Today, the canal is 120 miles (192 km) long. Its main channels are about 66 feet (20 m) deep and 985 feet (300 m) wide at the surface, and plans are in the works to enlarge it further.

Fees from the more than 15,000 ships that transit the canal every year bring Egypt

Cotton (right) was once one of Egypt's main sources of income, but today the Suez Canal brings in four times more revenue than cotton. Each year, eight percent of the world's sea trade passes through the canal. Despite its high traffic volume, the waterway sees few accidents, thanks to the convoy system (opposite).

almost $2 billion annually. Tankers carrying oil from the Middle East make up much of the canal's traffic. Other shipments include metals, grain, and coal. Warships and passenger liners also occasionally travel the canal.

Because most of the Suez Canal is wide enough for only one ship to travel at a time, ships must sail in **convoys**, much like the cars of a train. Every day, two convoys from the north and one from the south transit the canal. Departures are carefully timed so that north- and southbound ships meet at one of four passing points, where the canal widens.

The journey all the way through the canal takes an average of 14 hours.

With so much traffic passing from East to West and West to East through the Suez Canal, the waterway today continues to fulfill Ferdinand de Lesseps's dream of connecting two worlds. Although the statue of de Lesseps that once stood at the northern entrance of the canal has been destroyed by war, its Latin inscription, reflecting de Lesseps's intention for the canal, has been realized: *Aperire terram gentibus*, which means "To open the world to all people."

SEEING THE WONDER

The Suez Canal teems with life from the Mediterranean and Red Seas. Ranging from muddy to sandy, areas of the canal bottom support water plants. Fish such as rainbow sardines, mullets, sea bass, and bluefish make their home in the canal, as do several crab species.

Visitors to the northern end of the Suez Canal can view Port Said by ferry (opposite) or enjoy watching the area's birds, including pelicans (right).

The Suez Canal is often overlooked by tourists visiting Egypt, but a trip to this waterway can be a relaxing and rewarding way to spend a day. Most visitors to Egypt fly into Cairo. From Cairo, the canal can be reached via bus, train, taxi, or rental car. A road parallels the canal along its western bank and offers a close view of the water- way. Or, for an even closer view, tourists may embark on a cruise from Suez to Port Said.

Many visitors to the canal are struck by the contrast between its eastern and western shores. Barren sand dunes still dot most of the eastern shore, where there is no fresh water. The western shore, however, benefits from the Sweet Water Canal, and many of its cities have become resort towns. Both Port Said and Suez offer good views of ships traveling the canal. In Port Said, visitors can take a ferry ride across the waterway or enjoy a 90-minute lunch or dinner cruise on the canal. Nearby, the small islands of Lake Manzala offer unique bird-watching opportunities, with the chance to see fen birds, coots, pelicans, and flamingoes.

Ismailia is considered by many to be one of the most pleasant Egyptian cities.

Blinding sandstorms and thick fog occasionally limit visibility on the Suez Canal. In order to prevent accidents, ships entering the waterway must take experienced Suez Canal pilots onboard. The pilots are trained in a simulator that recreates dangerous conditions and emergency situations.

Featuring lush, vibrant gardens, charming colonial-style houses, and beautiful beaches, it is a popular place for water activities such as fishing, swimming, wind surfing, and jet skiing. All three of the major canal cities offer hotels of varying costs.

The best time to visit the Suez Canal is in the winter (November to March), when temperatures are cooler, averaging around 70 °F (21 °C) during the day. Visitors to Egypt should be aware, however, that prices tend to be higher during this time of year, and hotels are often booked. No matter what time of year one visits, a light sweater or jacket is recommended in the evening, when the desert becomes cool.

Foreigners need a passport and visa—documents that allow entrance into a country—to travel in Egypt. As is the case in other Middle Eastern nations, tourists should follow advice from local security authorities and respect local Muslim customs. Photography in Egypt is restricted in some places, including military and strategic sites, so travelers should be on the lookout for signs describing such restrictions.

Visitors to the Suez Canal are likely to be enchanted by its cities, including the charming buildings of Ismailia (top); its views, including sunsets colored by sand blowing through the air (opposite); and, of course, the canal itself, a true wonder of the modern world.

SUEZ  CANAL

QUICK FACTS

Location: Northeastern Egypt; the canal city of Suez is about 80 miles (130 km) east of Cairo

Time of construction: April 1859 to November 1869

Opening date: November 17, 1869; it was celebrated with bands, cannons, and an extravagant party in Ismailia as about 50 ships sailed the canal

Composition: Sand; most banks along the canal are reinforced with stone, cement, and steel

Engineer: Ferdinand de Lesseps

Work force involved: ~ 2.4 million laborers

Length: 120 miles (192 km)

Depth: ~ 66 feet (20 m) in the main channels

Width: ~ 985 feet (300 m) at surface level in the main channels

Cost to build: ~ $100 million

Funded by: The Egyptian government and French shareholders

Annual traffic: ~ 15,000 ships

Visitors per year: Statistics are not available due to the canal's great expanse

GLOSSARY

Bedouins — Arab people of the northern African desert who have no permanent home but move from place to place

cholera — a severe and often fatal disease caused by contaminated food or water

convoys — groups of vehicles, such as automobiles or ships, that travel together

copra — the dried meat of the coconut, from which coconut oil is obtained

diplomat — a person who represents his or her country in official relations with other countries

East — the part of the world that includes the countries of Asia

Industrial Revolution — a period in the 1700s and 1800s characterized by major advances in factories' technology, mainly in Europe

isthmus — a narrow strip of land connecting two larger land areas

Muslims — people who follow Islam, the religion in which believers worship one God, Allah, whose prophet is Mohammed

Ottoman Empire — a vast empire (control of many territories by one group) that lasted from 1300 to 1918; it was centered in modern-day Turkey and covered parts of Asia, Africa, and Europe

Persians — people from Persia (modern-day Iran); the Persian Empire, which covered southwest Asia, lasted from the sixth century B.C. until 331 B.C.

pharaohs — kings of ancient Egypt; pharaohs were worshipped as gods descended from the sun god, Ra

shares — equal parts into which a property or company owned by a number of people is divided; each person owns a certain number of shares, or percentage

viceroy — a person who rules a country as a representative of a "mother" country or empire

West — the part of the world that includes the countries of Europe and North America